95 at 95

95 at 95

A Life in Poems

Warren Lane Molton

Shanti Arts Publishing
Brunswick, Maine

95 at 95: A Life in Poems

Published by Shanti Arts Publishing

Designed by Shanti Arts Designs

Photograph of the author on the cover was taken by Stephen Molton and is used with his permission.

Shanti Arts LLC
193 Hillside Road
Brunswick, Maine 04011
shantiarts.com

Printed in the United States of America

ISBN: 978-1-956056-97-6

Library of Congress Control Number: 2023940935

To Mary Dian, my beloved wife of seventy-three years,
and to our three grown children and their mates:
Stephen and Pamela, Jennifer and Bruce,
and David and Jessica.

Contents

Foreword

The valedictory tributes from a child to a parent are apt to be presented simplistically, the fulsome reality of mixed emotions buried in gratitude. In writing this "Foreword," piecemeal through a time of personal trials, I've realized it's best to stay "in the Now," to resist the summations of hindsight and credit the poet as if he weren't going anywhere, even at age ninety-five. "The cow is now," as he writes herein, forever now as all good poetry should be. So, his children won't make a point of looking back here. We'll just give thanks that he's still alive as I write, with all our relationships' simplicity and complexity rolled into one.

In a recent film about the mysterious phenomenon of "quantum entanglement," a Viennese physicist ended it by remarking that he would like to sit down with God someday and ask, "What were you thinking?!" when the universe was made.

Albert Einstein, who was pointedly not a believer in a personalized God, once wrote something along similar lines:

> "The most beautiful emotion we can experience is the mystical. It is the sower of all true art and science. He to whom this emotion is a stranger . . . is as good as dead. To know that what is impenetrable to us really exists, manifesting itself to us as the highest wisdom and the most radiant beauty, which our dull faculties can comprehend only in their most primitive forms—this knowledge, this feeling is at the center of all true religiousness. In this sense, and in this sense only, I belong to the ranks of devoutly religious men."

These words span the spectrum that the poet, Warren Molton, has lived his life in. A former clergyman, professor, and psychotherapist, his journey has been deliberately both outward and inward for perhaps all his ninety-five years. We are each ourselves grounded in reality, even as we are parts of a vast, ineffable Oneness, and there lie the nearly unspeakable mysteries that poets try to speak of anyway.

He started writing in his teens. Raised in the deep South during the Great Depression, where whispers of lynchings on Saturday night could still be heard on church steps on Sunday morning, he has always been trying to reconcile history with eternity—the One and the All, the now and the forever, the good, the bad, and the ugly. A spiritual leader in a Navy town at the height of the Cold War, he was always looking for the language that could honor the courage of patriots even as he wondered aloud at the collective crime of war. As a minister, a healer, a spouse, and a father, he had only small scraps of time to try to understand his own existential search for the sacred. But his watch-phrase, even at his most godforsaken, always was and still is, "Nevertheless, I am," in all its wonder and brave perplexity.

Nevertheless, we are, even if God is no more.

For decades, Molton has traversed his sense of wonder, his fascination at the ephemeral nature of life, love, loss, anger and anguish, memory and expectation, even as he wandered away from the explicitly religious. He would say that he didn't leave the church, that the church left him. Or perhaps its walls just vaporized, its poetry fulfilling itself in the individual quest, in action.

"Only when I got to the point where I couldn't find God anywhere, did I start to see God everywhere . . ." this poet once told his agnostic oldest son.

Poetry is soul work, as he practices it, a kind of spiritual sonar, taking soundings of the Self as it enters and exits the deep.

Is there or is there not a conscious universe? His work is always asking; always preoccupied with the question of why there is something instead of nothing; with questions of autonomy and belonging; of the place of our consciousness within what might or might not be a void of greater meaning.

It's a perilous time for poets, as I write. No one writes anything until they can cast off Harold Bloom's "anxiety of influence," and just now there are suddenly "apps" that want to do our writing for us. It's essential that we keep poetry ours, even when our machines start to think that they can mimic us "perfectly." A poem is an echo of a flesh-and-blood life. No machine will find meaning for us, no matter how well they learn to mimic us. It will never rightly know what it is to be human at its best or worst. We find our meaning in our doing. The unassailable value of the likes of Viktor Frankl, the Holocaust survivor's assertion of meaning as the mind's utmost purpose, is echoed in Molton's work, as well; the need to make a presence from the absence; to populate the vast emptiness that seems to surround this Earth of ours. And if the emptiness is indeed empty, then we can at least comfort and challenge and delight in using poetry to protect each other from the despair that might well fill that void if we let it.

As with Edward Hopper and so many other American artists in the Emersonian mode, there is still magic to be found in everyday life. Once you find that magic, however fleetingly, the phrase will never feel like a trope again.

Circumstances have required that I write this while on the road, "falling forward" as Emerson prescribed. This morning, I thought I'd find a quiet spot to finish it in the lobby of a Best Western motel, pre-dawn, in Weatherford, Oklahoma, but no sooner did I find a place just beyond the Muzak and sit down to write, than a lady with Downs Syndrome and a proud, beatific smile came up to me to tell me that the complimentary breakfast was prepared and ready for me, and a duet of women singing hymns in Spanish rose from behind the floor-to-ceiling fireplace. When I went back to the buffet to refill my coffee cup, I discovered it was just one Latina singing along with a congregation she had pulled up on her iPhone before her workday began, and she glanced at me and turned it down.

"No," I said, "Keep singing. It's beautiful," and with a shy grin she resumed her song of praise with the disembodied choir on the tiny screen in front of her. In other words, God (or something quite like it) was everywhere, filling every attempt I made to hear myself think.

My father left America for some twenty months when I was three to serve as a U.S. Army chaplain in Korea when the war there was nearing its end. All I had of him were the episodic stories of a cowboy named Coconut Bill that he'd write and draw in letter form and send me from the frontlines. That was the essence of our relationship during those formative months in this kid's life, but they were alive and intimately mine enough to keep our relationship bright and meaningful. The poetry is wherever you can find it and perhaps you will find it here, as I found it in an envelope sealed and sent from a tent on the other side of the world.

This book is not all "about God," nor is it a work that bends toward the ascetic. It's not a way to remove yourself from history, from the life of the body in time, from the senses, from love and power and the confrontation between them that becomes justice or enslavement. These are the soundings of an active and applied faith in faith itself to surmount the depravities that still mar the human experience. It's a reminder that we must act in good faith all the time, whatever our beliefs. This is the record of a lifelong attempt to connect the immaterial with the material for the betterment of both.

And in your own way, at your own pace, you might find some epiphanies here yourself, some new inroads to meaning, discovered on your own terms.

One can only hope.

Stephen Molton
On the road in Weatherford, Oklahoma
April 30, 2023

Acknowledgments

Again, to my dear wife who always saw my poems first and was insightful with her critique.

Also recognized for their work in bringing this book to fruition are:

. . . my daughter-in-law Jessica, who organized and prepared the full body of my work for editorial review and selection by my daughter, Jennifer, whom I also recognize for her contribution to this project,

. . . my son Stephen, liaison in the publication management of this book with Christine Brooks Cote of Shanti Arts Publishing,

. . . my son David, for his sheer presence in my life, and

. . . my best buddy, Bob Price, who at every breakfast meeting would ask, "Okay, what's the latest poem?"—discussion of which often consumed the length of our time together.

Special thanks to Jill Baumgaertner, poetry editor of *The Christian Century* where over thirty of my poems have appeared since 1956.

There are countless others who have read my poems for years and encouraged me along the way.

Lastly, I'd like to mention Presbyterian pastor, retired senior minister of the historic First Presbyterian Church of New York, and literary friend, Barry Shepherd. Also a poet published in *The Christian Century,* Barry and I often swapped poems before they were submitted for publication.

The poems that begin with "If God Is" come from my book *If God Is: A Poetic Search for God Within,* published in 2002 by Forest of Peace Books. These poems (pages 39–51, 53–59, 107, 111, 124, 127, and 128) were written at a time in my life when I couldn't find God anywhere and began to see God everywhere.

The following poems previously appeared in *New Poems, 2004–2012* (CreateSpace Publishing, 2012):
"A Friend's Dream on Good Friday";
"Christmas Is Available Space";
"Dialogue";
"Going Home to Be Born";
"I Mourn My Own Dream Unicorn";
"Life Signs";
"Moon Prints";
"Seagull";
"Shine"; and
"Speaking of Great Choirs."

The following poems previously appeared in *Bruised Reeds* (Judson Press, 1970):
"A Living Place";
"A Peddler's Prayer";
"Black Man";
"Mystery Play";
"Paper Bells";
"Prayer from the Steeple";
"Seminary Commencement";
"Small Miracle";
"Toyhood Prayer of a Man"; and
"Who Called?"

Surrender Years

These are our surrender years:
Giving back, giving forward,
Giving up—
Old debts paid, new gifts given,
Favors rewarded and questions
Of soul given dialogue with mercy.

These are our surrender years:
Full of old dreams revisited,
Lost dreams excused,
New dreams adrift with beguiling smiles
And truth standing by, not because
But just in case.

These are our surrender years,
Lean with wear, tough with time,
And faithful with forgiveness.

These are our surrender years:
Still thankful with humor,
Generous with hope,
And rich with bountiful love.

Alarm Cock

The rooster acts as though appointed
  and regally anointed
  divine booster of the sun.
When most of us would just as soon
  let Sol sleep in,
  the rooster rises at first light
  crowing his comb crimson
  with manifest delight.
In fact, he's sure that night
  just might last forever if he
  refused to rise and shine
  in the nick of time.
From Knob Noster to Brewster
  while many of us make breakfast,
  the rooster makes a rude awakening
  and ruins many an attitude
  all down the longitude—
  while busy in the dawning
  making morning.
So,
  unlike this Herald of Helios, Hyperion and Ra,
  and day-breaker chanticleer,
  some of us have joined the Early Risers Club
  and by the clock make sure we rise
  before this noisy cock,
  this loudmouth rooster
  even if we are usta
  going to bed with the chickens;
  and we can take the guff of sleepyheads
  who say we're just braggarts showing of,
  but it's still fun to be the one
  who now wakes the one up
  who thinks he wakes the sun up.

Almost All the Way

When my mother knew that she was dying,
she asked my father not to call the children.
"It's Christmas and I don't want to make a fuss.
I'll see them by and by," she said. Her pastor
and three deacons came and stood around her bed,
begging her to go to the hospital.
She only smiled and said, "This is best,"
and when they were at last alone, my father slipped
into bed beside her and held her while her
body slowly cooled, and they filled the day
with sweet memories as he went with her
all the way to the gates.

An Old Vet Remembers His Soldier Pines

Friends never hailed me captain when a child,
So I withdrew, and pledged myself the chief
Of half-a-hundred companies of pines.
There were no envious whines of discontent,
But rather just a soft and whispered sigh
As though they placed implicit trust in me.

My army stalwart stood in rigid pose
Heeding every word of my command;
No traitor's clamor of objection rose:
"See Green Cedarland across the way?
Conquer the land! We'll pay the bloody fee."

Breezes nudged the boughs to sloppy salute,
Then I proceeded all alone to cast
My cone-grenades across the boundary creek
And cried aloud my own explosive, "Boom."
We only shelled this way and dared no raids.

Now the battle of the trees is won.
Infiltrating pines could never shun their task.
They, as instructed, took Green Cedarland,
And year by year the persevering pines,
Like an occupying army, still root out the enemy.

Today, they wave to me and parent-pines,
Who never crossed the separating stream;
And I still wonder if some day another boy
Will lead these trees, with his own youthful dream,
Across the hill to fill the rolling land,
The open, flowing fields with soldier pines.

Chimp

Chimp, you imp,
  elf in the evolutionary tree,
I see no clear solution
  for you and me, no answer
  for the wonder in our eyes
  as we meet,
  nor to my wondering about the ties
  we have long shared
  in our wandering together,
  the weather of welcome between us,
  the mystery of our small surprises,
  your gestures after me,
  mine that pretend to interpret you
  while polishing the mirror of our laughter
  only to find the empty smile.
Still,
  you are in our constellation
  peering into our faces
  across light years of separation.
Chimp,
  even without all the graces,
  if your heart is only half as moved
  for me as mine for you,
  distances dissolve between us,
  as I reach out to you, my friend,
  our kin.

Autumn

Each year every tree in Brookside is different.
Yellows tones and hues I know I've
  never seen before,
  and scarlet, pixilated white on greens,
  gold of every denomination, small round
  coins of color, and banana-yellow fingers
  on trees I never named.
And that is a Pignut Hickory, she says,
  showing off, pointing to a great splash
  of yellow and green.
One lonely spruce stands tall in its own
  climate of ripe fall fragrance.
An oak still green with one small spray
  of tan, as though to say, I know, I know.
  Just wait.
A covey of black birds light and leave
  a raked-clean yellowing lawn.
Canada geese are honking through
  a traffic of puffy clouds nowhere close.
And, there, suddenly before us
  a swirl of leaves in the street
  wanting to fly along.
Our walk is brief, slowed by years, as we
  mellow toward winter.
Why don't we go inside, she says, out of the
  chill and build a fire, make cocoa, sit close
  and smell the smoke and pretend we're
  as young as we were when we found our
  home forty-two years ago.

Bear

A bear empties the air,
  defines *beware,*
  looks regal and omnipotent
  as an opponent.
When we try to bring bears down to size.
We stuff and make them soft and small enough
  for children to squeeze and cuddle while dozing off.
  We name them Teddy, Winnie, Smokey,
  and Pooh Bear, or some other friendly name,
  but never Fatty or Skinny or Hokey.
So, Grizzly, Polar, Kodiak and Koala,
  are to glacier and tree
  as lion to Africa
  whale to sea
  and eagle to air
  yet...seeing them, we can only stare.
Standing statuesque
  all head and fur
  great paws and claws,
  or locked in place as hunter
  with its great mouth open
  and looking fine
  with sheen and shine
  in some mountain stream
  brimmed with salmon or trout.
Bear is nature's high priest
  a monarch crowned.
We share the Earth with giants.

Black Man

God,
I did not see him fall,
yet I am sure he fell.
For I have missed his thick call,
his long flat stride around the town
and tall dark stretch
above entitled whites.
His death within my hollow day
might be forgotten,
except I know you saw
though I did not.
And I have missed his final fling
against the veined sky
and where his last prayer leapt.
I pray to remember
the way he walked among us
poised and black.
Amen.

Dialogue

The call
  to the rise
                          and fall
  of it all
The answering question
  shift   and   scoot
  cinch and pinch
  up   and   back
  seeking
                  gravity's
                    center
The playful twist
  and turn
  slipping and sliding
  with bursts   of laughter
  in the up
               and down
  and bounce
The need
  to find and keep rhythm
                    with the other
  riding the fulcrum
The search to stay in sync
                          with the face
  and leveling eyes
         size
              and balance and pace
The surge and flow and range
  and reach
  of stop   and   go

The changing tides
  on both sides
  from center
The steadying energy
  of each
The slowing
  stopping
  and dropping
  together
  off the see-saw.

Christmas Is Available Space

Christmas is her small womb
  seeded,
  slowly growing, grooming
  for a glorious universe
  assembling yet again
  and eternally
  in woman.
Christmas here makes
  room enough for soul,
  living space for the sacred
  arriving as life codes
  on finger tips,
  as color infuses eyes,
  as names are promised,
  and all that is left
  is for mother and child
  to ride out an awful emptying,
  for this new child to cry out,
  to gasp, to breathe,
  to empty and be filled
  again and again
  with the holiest of spirits—
  the breath of this green Earth,
  mother of gods,
  still amazingly able
  to empty us with dread
  and fill us with awe.

Ecologists

The Amish keep heaven
   in hay-spill stacks,
Seven sweets and seven sours,
Scythes and reapers heap
   the racks,
Honey wheat and clover towers.
They bonnet the sun and sip
   the rains,
Seven droughts and seven showers,
Seeders and dungers march
   the lanes,
Fruit the trees and grape the bowers.
They hive the bees and gourd
   the birds,
Seven herbs and seven flowers,
Grow barnyard prayers without
   any words,
Death is mine, and life is ours.

Going Home to Be Born

Vacationing in Florida thirty years ago,
my wife, Dian, and I drove one Sunday morning
two hours north to my birthplace in Floral City.
Over the years, the story I heard was that I was born
at home in a small summer lake cottage where
my family lived, awaiting a larger house and me.
For nearly a mile, we entered the town down
a street canopied with sun-dappled water oaks
lavishly draped with great strands of Spanish moss.
We quickly found the lake and parked in front of one
of a half dozen white cottages gathered at the head
of a rutted dirt road leading down to the water.
As I got out of the car, I saw half of a blue bird's
shell open on the grass at my feet. I smiled and left
it there, but caught its special greeting.
We took the path to the lake my mother said she had
walked each evening to encourage my birth,
and after a few moments of tribute at the lakeside,
we hugged, kissed and walked back wondering
which cottage had been my first home.
As we approached the car, a woman drove up,
greeted us and asked if she could be of help.
I told her my story of being born in one of the
cottages and that we had returned on a sentimental
journey. She exclaimed, "You were born right
here in the cottage where you parked. Your brothers
were my playmates," and she called their names.
"Do you want to see inside?" Of course we did.
And we walked into the cathedral of my birth.
She stood back to allow us to wander silently together
in our dream. "I live here in summer," she said softly.
Four rooms and a sleeping porch for my brothers.

When I found myself at the foot of an old iron-frame bed,
our guide, standing in the doorway, spoke again
softly, "You were born one morning in that very bed."
I had and have no words, only a sense of a mother's mystery
finding her voice in a mellow pitched contralto of praise
when the doctor said, "It's another boy, Mrs. Molton."
Back at our condo in the early evening, we strolled the quiet
beach alone, but for an old man in a lawn chair smoking
his pipe. And when I picked up a small white conch shell,
seeing what I had found, he called, "You don't find those
here anymore. You got yourself a keeper." And so I do.

Funky Skunk

After my walk in the woods,
  I decided not
  to write a poem
  about this weasel family punk
  who so long ago
  should have slunk
  off and become a critter monk,
  instead of dunking
  folks like me in his despicable way
  with a spray
  of his funky musk
  that stuck to me
  like a spatter of gunk
  and the tree trunk
  I shrunk behind
  trying to escape his junk
  that leaves me now in such a funk.
I flunk
  when it comes to the skunk
  as you can tell,
  but it's just as well
  since most of the words that rhyme
  with skunk
  stink.

He Descended into Hell

This unlikely tomb
    this once plundered vault
    this meager poke of broken power
    this moldy hole at the foothills
    of Zion and the soul
    this piddling down to fissure and fault
    this dry womb
    delivered us the earth angel
    Jes-us
    just like us
    only wanting out more than in
    yet staying there long enough
    to cup one last beatitude
    for those in ruin
    and touch the tongues of hell's angels
    on his way here.

Horse of Course

Muscular, mystical, mythical force,
and one is of three creatures
we've groomed away from the wild
along with the dog and cat
into that great human circle
of Adam, Eve and the Child,
even though with each new foal
we must raise them with the goal
of breaking the hold of the wilderness
in order to tame each one we bridle and name.
Shakespeare's King Richard offered
his kingdom for a horse,
and Lady Godiva rode
through the streets of Coventry
wearing nothing and risking divorce
on her high-flanked horse.

Workhorse, racehorse, warhorse
define our centuries of partnership.
The smallest jockey takes on grace
in a race astride his horse.
Conquering heroes are raised to new heights
on this dancing, prancing, majestic beast;
while in the funeral cortege,
the horse without its rider is a solemn reminder
of the people's grief at the loss of the deceased.
The horse is a great symbolic force and very *Yang*,
a strong man's beast;
but with its sensitivity and delicate response, very *Yin*,
for women.
Descended to us from Chiron, Unicorn and Pegasus,
equestrians all, and our partner in it all—
the noble horse, of course.

Hungry and You Fed Me,
Naked and You Clothed Me

She must have hopped off the open boxcar of a freight train
pulling slowly into the yards at Macon. She looked it
when my mother let her in at the back door just as we
    sat down
to supper. Mother usually fed hobos at the back door,
but this one she invited inside to join the family.

It was a cool October night and she wore a cotton dress
with a lavender print, and without speaking, she bowed
with prayer-hands to us all. At my mother's suggestion
she sat next to me on the bench. After grace we began
to eat, and most unlike our family, no one spoke.

I was seven and shy, but turned quickly once to
    glimpse her wrinkled
face lined with dark ruts from who knows how many
    days on the road.
She ate faster than we, offering prayer hands with
    every few bites.
Finishing, she took another roll from the basket,
stuffed it in the pocket of her dress, and stood, bowing
to us again as she turned to leave. My mother rose
to follow her. Speaking with her at the door, my mother said
with a note of scold, *It's cold out there.* When she returned
to the table, she no longer wore her old blue sweater.

If God Is a Circle

If God is a circle
    whose center is everywhere,
    the saint dwells at the center
    and guards the well
    from which the water of all life flows,
    plants the garden that surrounds the well,
    tends the trees of life and love,
    while the poet lives at the edge of the circle,
    moving back and forth
    from the world to the well,
    troubling the saint with questions
    and filling his pitcher with water
    for the world left at the edge;
    and the people say how sweet the water is,
    how cold, how fresh and clear.
Then
    on some fateful night or day,
    when the moon is blood
    or the sun is in eclipse,
    the water turns to wine,
    and the poet calls the saint
    away from guarding the well
    and they drink and dance with the people
    who laugh and cry out words
    of thanksgiving and praise;
    yet, like children before sleep,
    their ecstasy turns to anger
    as they hang the poet upon a tree
    while the saint is taken to his well
    and drowned,

just as some pilgrim saint
comes down from the hills
to clear the well once more
and a wandering poet arrives
with a new wineskin.

If God Is My Great Ivied Wall

If God is my great ivied wall,
  gray in winter
  when laminating ice and snow
  stick against the stone
  and a pale sun
  luminates the trail
  of leaves that keep lifting
  until they now hang
  out along the top
  like bewildered green snakes;
Then
  we have arrived here
  together, God,
  where I too ran out of wall
  swaying in my soul's vertigo
  and searching for a firm next rock
  on which to land
  and gain a purchase
  for the last leg of a climb
  we began so long ago
  on what then seemed to me
  to be solid ground;
But now—
  and I can take a dare—
  are you suggesting
  that I must climb solely
  on the strength of the vine
  into thin air?

If God Is Even Somehow My Song

If God is even somehow my song,
as in the childish poems I sang
and the poems I left behind
in the bright woods budding
like Christmas lights in April;

If God is even somehow my song,
as in the poems I composed and quickly forgot
with the sudden rising of twin eagles
from their pinnacle pine,
lifting away like a ransom for me
toward the great snow-geese marsh;

If God is even somehow my song,
as in the poems I scribble down
or the ones I leave printed
in the sand as gulls and pipers
scatter before me alongside
the incoming tide;

If God is somehow my song
even in the dream-poems
I wake from with my heart breaking
and in tears for their missed, lost,
sleeping elegance, now homely and naive
in the naked morning light,

Then
I must keep wrestling with the Word
if I am to find my words,
and listening for God's song
if I am to sing.

If God Is Any Great Returning

If God is any great returning,
a listening to some new witness
bidding within,
any hard going back
to where in a rootless time
you quit,
as Bonhoeffer left life in New York
to return to his death in a Nazi prison,
so that now it's your turn
at the bitter feast of eating crow,
saying I'm sorry
to every cynical hello
after your selfish goodbye;

If God is any great returning,
your soul's yearning,
lonely and longing
for the path lost or deserted,
the cause dropped in its infancy
as too childish, too hard, too frail,
too sure to fail to bother,
but now somehow the only way
worthy of your life,
your death;

If God is any great returning,
and your burning soul
has spun your compass about
so that you are finally en-route home
like the prodigal,
then go quickly
expecting to feast with the Father
even though your whining brother
may not yet dine with you
and in truth
awaits proof, even as he should,
that you are really home
for good.

If God Is That Sublime Moment

If God is that sublime moment
in the story when Jesus said,
"And his father seeing him afar off . . ."
which could mean, of course,
that he had been watching every day for years,
longing for him,
straining to see him afar off—
it's that *afar off* that moves me;

or perhaps he only watched
in the late afternoon
thinking his son might try to get home before dark,
or early in the morning
after pressing on all through the night,
or at high noon
when his father stood
shadowless under the sun
and remembered his son's
innocence and sweetness;

or perhaps it was just by chance
he would see him
when he looked up
from repairing a harness
or tying a new broom
or from a nap in his favorite chair,
suddenly there he was,
his lost son
coming home . . .

or perhaps he only saw him
because it was his birthday—
his,
not his son's—
when his eldest,
forgetting the persistence of an old man's dream,
said, "Make a wish, Father,"
and he did
and looked up . . .
seeing him afar off.

If God Is This Bonsai Tree

If God is this bonsai tree,
  burnt-orange leaves
  igniting in the October sun
  of my florist's window . . .
  and here miniature
  in leaf and limb,
  trunk and root,
  marooned in a potter's dish;
If God is this ancient bonsai
  trapped like me
  in an earthen vessel,
  going through the motions
  of his seasons, sunrise-sunset,
  in his own sweet rule of time,
  dwarfed
  but ever budding, blooming toward
  an autumn burning;
Then
  I pause
  before his emblem flame
  that God might light my soul
  like a Moses bush,
  that I might keep seasons with him
  without a doubt
  and not burn out.

If God Is This Fearful Wind

If God is this fearful wind
  spinning in from the open sea
  with a Sinai voice commanding
  our wet gray beach to batten down
  and drunken sea oats to dance
  on the dunes like dervishes gone mad;
If God is this fearful wind
  talking in tongues
  across our deck, under eaves
  and down our flutey chimney:
    Trust but take cover,
    Believe but button down,
    Pray but ponder leaving;
If you, God, are this fearful wind
  howling in my soul,
  I must ride you out
  since you leave me no retreat,
  not even some neat formula to predict
  velocity, direction or possible damage;
  still,
  our voices wrangle in the wind . . .
  yours, God, and mine,
  and in our whirlwind of tongues
  I answer you:
    Remember, God,
    you are on your way
    while I must stay,
    so blow and go,
    as I await that great calm
    hiding,
    riding like a rainbow
    on your tail.

If God Is a Clown

If God is a clown working the crowd
    of this three-ring circus
    and letting himself be chased around
    by a toothless old tiger called Satan,
    and, with a single stroke
    of his paper-tassel whip
    and a puff of smoke, he makes Satan
    magically disappear through a trap door
    into the crackling hell
    of a sawdust pit;
If God is clowning with me,
    setting me on his knee
    and with lollipops and balloons
    telling me that all is well,
    only to drop me
    through that same trap door
    into a hell of merely dying;
If, indeed, God in Christ is clowning,
    setting reality on its ear
    with a gospel hard to hear
    that the weak are strong,
    the meek inherit the earth,
    and with faith in him and new birth
    even death means life eternal,
    only to let me sleep that great sleep
    forever . . .
Well then,
    what a circus this has been,
    and how I've loved
    the lions, tigers and bears,
    the dancing elephants and calliope,
    even the bazooka band
    and the high-wire acts
    with all those shining faces looking up;

But, oh that major-domo,
that solitary clown
who loved us children so,
who soothed our fears
and made us laugh with joy to tears
and feel loved . . .
I shall dream of him
forever.

If God Is This Rattler

If God is this rattler
  I am stripping
  off its skin
  when I am ten,
  pulling with mouse-nose
  pliers at the hide
  along the beads
  of blood
  beneath his head
  on down each side and over a carcass
  fit now only for a meal
  to brag about,
  down finally
  to the rattling end
  of his last shedding
  as green flies
  swarm
  at the awful head
  hammered
  with nails
  to my favorite tree,
Then
  that must be
  why I will find
  I can never climb
  this tree
  again
  or drive nails
  through any bark.

Mystery Play

Lord,
This cup
came down through the years:
mother, grandmother,
and a few generations
before them
used it to measure
flour and sugar.
Mother spoke of grimacing through
her first dose
of castor oil in coffee
from this cup.
I planted a single hyacinth
in it last fall
and kept it hidden
in the cellar all winter.
This spring I took it out
and set it in the sun,
where it grew and blossomed
into a fragrant, lovely thing
that caught the eye
of my two year old
who loved it from the window
to the floor.
The cup is broken,
the flower bruised and torn.
The church is that cup,
Christ that hyacinth,
and I am that child.

If God Is Running Water

If God is running water,
first blood of all creation,
dripping now from pipe and faucet
rising like a mantis
praying for rain
at a village watering spigot
in Ethiopia;
If God is running water
diving as the falls at Victoria,
or creeping through the cracks of sewers
in crumbling cities everywhere,
or Old Faithful spouting predictably,
or dropping from the sparkling black brow
of a diamond miner in South Africa;
If God is that awful tide that runs
against the polluting affairs of man,
water splitting the Red Sea,
water issuing from the rock under Moses' rod,
water swaddling Jesus in the Jordan,
water that is most of the blood of the Lamb,
water seeping into the sod
at the foot of the cross;
If God is water coursing through my body,
then I am a desert
and she is my oasis soul fed by her spring
growing and spreading
as my last hope
under yet another burning day
of cloudless skies.

If God Is a Circle Closing

If God is a circle closing,
  reaching around wide like a lover's
  all-embracing arms,
  hands now fingertips apart,
  needing only to touch
  to make all things complete,
  brokenness healed,
  left hand finally knowing the right,
  alpha reaching omega;
Then I pray
  that the hiatus of God's hands
  might not yet close,
  for it is in that awkward place,
  the space between his hands,
  just small enough for me to hide,
  where the breach would be bridged,
  that God grows my soul.

If God Is This Smoky Fire

—after eye surgery

If God is this smoky fire
in the cave of my right eye,
this flame darting, flirting
with the wet sparkle of walls
wanting the flare of spring's
daffodil and forsythia yellows,
pear whites and tulip tree lavenders,
settling now as though in the dead
of winter for shades and shadows,
snow-glare, early dark,
driven back inside
to the ashy, leftover coals of winter
in the first week of spring;
Then
be here with me in this cave, God,
my back to trickling walls,
feet to your fire's soft glow,
and let us talk until morning;
and perhaps in your burning
will be the fire I need
to set this place ablaze with light
to last this winter of my darkness,
through this sad season
until the fountain fire of summer.
Speak God,
for you are in this catacomb with me
and we only leave together.
If I don't go, neither do you,
and if I leave we go rejoicing.

If God Is Content in His Own Forming

If God is content in his own forming,
  and recalls in a redemptive time
  what contrasts we also carry, and lets
  our quest lie down with questions
  beneath his anointing hands;
If God is content in his own forming,
  blessing each of us apart or near,
  allowing every soul its own journey
  now needing none to worship him
  or fear his hand;
If God is content in his own forming,
  confessing hunger for our trust,
  wanting our faces to light his darkness,
  yearning to rest within our graces
  though we be slipping from his hands;
If God is content in his own forming,
  and rising to the names we gave him,
  I wait for him to find his voice
  in some new sound beyond commandment,
  pure as the praise of our clapping hands;
If God is content in his own forming,
  I'm content to embrace my own,
  and accept his half-life, half-death gift
  as Christ did at his lonely going out,
  and deliver my own still-growing doubt
  into God's still-forming hands.

If God Is the Living Moment

If God is the living moment,
this one—now and now and ever now
without memory or history
or time moving away into artifacts,
moments caught in the mind's need
to fix itself somewhere in the flood
measured not by clocks,
calendars or carbon
but in one full moment of knowing—*now!*
If God is this living moment,
empty beyond now,
with no future, no grand plan
or map, but just light enough
for the space to the end of sight,
eye-speed to that star,
no more, no less,
not a maybe or what if, but indeed
a *now* where I keep breathing God
in, never out;
the going out is me dying, becoming *then,*
and *there* and *once,*
But God enters now,
God only enters now,
and now,
and Now!

If God Is the Artist

If God is the artist
beyond all comparing,
daring to compose earth's music
with only nature's sounds,
painting sunsets no one could afford,
sculpting human figures that never bored
anyone no matter how long
they might stand perfectly still;
If God is the artist
who carves diamonds in beauty's eyes,
who is the spectrum itself
from which all colors came,
poet of poets beyond name and fame,
dreaming dreams into flesh;
If God is the artist of us all,
I search for God's signature
somewhere on me
that might sign me as authentic masterpiece,
one of God's eternal treasures,
priceless and a true measure of the artist,
a monument now and always;
Oh well,
perhaps God's tattoo,
these words,
will do.

If God Is to Be My Last Rite of Passage

If God is to be my last rite of passage,
  dry Camel's Eye,
  Way through Kafka's castle wall
  or Blake's heaven's gate,
  or even Alice's door for goodness sake,
  last stalled-out toll booth
  where I surrender all my brassy tokens,
  pride's pocket change
  picked up along the way
  from seems-like-only-yesterday
  down to that last tight squeeze
  through the needle's eye
  at that vexed exit
  where I could both end
  and begin again;
If God is the slit in the curtain
  that I slip through, certain
  that this *adieu* to lights
  and bright faces, polite applause,
  cat calls or bravo is but the final pause,
  bow, wave and goodnight,
  only to enter upon a fairer stage
  with familiar faces on the other side
  of this divide;
Then
  I shall enter quite amazed
  and stammering about how thrilled
  I am to be here . . . there . . . anywhere,
  everywhere,
  at last.

I Mourn My Own Dream Unicorn

From whence have you come, my unicorn,
  Your head a silver moon,
And where did you find your lofty crown
  That horn of holy rune?

What smithy forged your flinty shoes
  Of platinum and gold
To catch the burning rays of sun
  Yet match the star's deep cold?

And from what treasure chest your eyes
  Lit at the ruby's core,
What angel wove your Pegasus wings
  On what imagined shore?

Is there no way to bid you stay
  Or catch with paint or pen?
Can I write the poem that will stir my soul
  Into dreaming you back again?

In the deepest part of me
  Where only dreams survive,
You, my unicorn, must live
  Until you are alive.

Leaving for Home

They called him king, laughing.
He called for water and got it
spiked with vinegar.
They taunted, begged and he
promised them a splendid arrival.
They did their killing, and he
forgave their ignorance.
He watched them gamble for his
pitiful garments.
Imagine slipping his robe
around your shoulders,
his sandals on your feet.
His mother who once thought
him crazy and came early
to take him home, he gave
to a friend like a good son.
He tidied up his earthliness
before leaving.

Then it hit him: *Eloi, Eloi,*
Abba Father, where in this hell
are you?
Out of the lost years, finally
the cry of the child:
Abba, forbidden for servants,
but a child could call his daddy.
Such plunging darkness gathering.
His holy of holies shattered, blasted,
leaving nothing . . .
then maybe something—
the surely somewhere waiting hands
of the absent one,
and his own right to go
with dignity.

He called for curtain.
It was over, done, finished
And left with his earlier promise
  to prepare a place,
  arms out, inviting.

Cat

My cat,
in her life's task of grooming
knows every path of bone and fur,
every wing of bent light flickering on her
as she flexes to her tongue's busy task,
then rises up and simply sits
knowing she is clean.
She is at once a marvelous machine
knowing how to throttle down
to my human hand,
and yet a grand design of life
stalking here and there
then suddenly darting
into some imagined eternity.
She does not know what I know
or even what I know of her,
yet, like most kin of her kingdom,
seems to know more than we think she knows
of everything, without even knowing that.

Life Prisoner

If God is my guard
  and I his life prisoner
  then I must contest my guilt
  and the case of charges
  built against me
  from Adam and Eve's indictment
  down through courts and councils
  created or commandeered
  by Paul, Augustine, Aquinas,
  and the long line of Church Fathers,
  martyred to their own machinations;
Even as I remain captive
  making miracles in my mind:
    flesh of bread
    blood of wine
  in an awful flood of transmutations
  until guard gentles to guardian
  and prisoner is commuted to
  pastor, prophet and priest.

Love Is Everywhere

There is no place where love is not,
  and although this seems like a double negative,
  sounds like a plot, a Gordian knot,
  and is easier said than believed,
  it rings true, feels good,
  even theological like *Word of God:*
  all of that, and that's a lot,
  still there is no place where love is not.

Yet, we live like fish
  swimming around in search of water,
  a blind mole pressing on to find soil,
  or an olive its oil—absurd, like a bird
  flying about without a care looking for air.
No, love is everywhere, yet such a paradox!

For still we must look for love around the bend,
  over the rainbow and across this room,
  or that street, on the other side of an argument;
  near or far we must search for love,
  knowing it is hard to find sometime,
  but hardest of all when love is finally found,
  for then we must nurture it and help it grow,
  then be prepared to let it go.

So if we are born, bathed and buried
  in love, you and I have no excuse
  not to be God's lovers in the world,
  all of us all the time; and today can be
  our Renewal Day, starting right here
  where we are by first loving ourselves
  and taking small loving steps toward others,
  as holy others, and on to every living creature
  all the way to God.

For it is with the eye of love that we find God,
  and the eye of love that God finds us.
What a lovely way to live,
  and, of course, the only way to die.

Looking for Light in a Dark Time

It's dark along the way that I must go.
I do not like this road and would gladly trade
with any number of men I know.
I have tried making lights.
I found my old flashlight,
bought a new bulb and replaced the dry cells.
I call it Poor Excuse. It's usually dim.
Once I even brought down a forgotten
old milk glass oil lamp from the attic
and managed to find a decent light with it.
Fifty years ago we kept it near in case of storms,
but in recent years the power lines
have been better at holding on.
I call this lamp Grandpa Thomas.
He was a good and pious man
who never complained of darkness.
Once, our small son suggested
catching a million fireflies,
putting them in a fruit jar
and setting the whole business
on the porch to light the steps.
But of course none of these will do.
I need a light that cannot be carried
in a man's hand or lit or kept around just in case.
I need a light that does not depend on eyes.

Unlucky Duck

On October eleven, nineteen seventy-seven
 the *CBS Morning News* carried the story
 of the Tokyo zoo's drake duck crippled
 by a predator, then ostracized by the other ducks
 because he was disabled.

Ducks fly in flocks, mate for life, but not with cripples.
 The other ducks refused to let him drink or eat,
 swim or sleep with them, and if he came close,
 they honked and fluttered until he went away.
 He became the proverbial pariah, driven out,
 unwanted and despised.

Desperate then to find a friend, the drake dragged
 himself every day from the feeder to the edge
 of the fishpond, where he scattered pellets
 of duck food in the water's edge for the fish
 who waited daily for his gift.

Moon

"Go out on a starry night
and look up, then close
your eyes and realize
it is just as vast inside."
—Carl Jung

Under this night sky
I remember once more
how every creature
that ever looked up has seen her
in awe and wonder,
a lover's lunacy,
expecting moonlight
to be there always
to gentle the night.
Now
still spinning with us
Earth's balance wheel
shifting tidal wombs
of seas and menses,
floats there
insisting
that I keep striking fire,
with mere words
to light my way.

Oak

Our Oak is the mast under which we sail.
It is more properly known as a pin-oak,
  whose leaf-lobes are toothed and pointed,
  with deep, irregular sinuses extending nearly
  to the midrib, bearing almost round, brownish
  acorns by the bushels.
In spring
  its leafy sails are hoisted slowly over our decks,
  billowing full and green to catch
  the slightest breeze simpering through
  to tease, or again, gusting as though to sink us.
One October morning as I took my walk
  under neighborhood oaks along our village streets,
  an acorn, perched above me, let go, fell,
  hit the sidewalk, bounced once and sprang into
  the illusive moving target of that subtle space
  between my cuff and wrist, and lodged there
  as though begging like a waif to be taken in.
Today, like a rare precious seed,
  it nestles in a clutch
  of small sea shells on my desk
  awaiting one improbable last-chance journey
  toward becoming its own towering mast
  rising in its rigging and determined to sail.

Off the Coast of Charleston

For decades, Wild Dunes was our vacation home
until aging with the sea and sand and shifting
with the dunes and the wash of waves,
we surrendered as our beach, too, sifted away.
On our last morning walk with a gritty wind
at our backs, a covey of gulls no longer
amusing us with their squawking laughs
squatted sleek and silent like sentinels
facing into the wind.

And we won't forget the old man on his cane who
stopped us to say, "Hey, you know the ocean's
moving in to stay, and I just pray the good Lord
will give us a Moses who can do the math
and to hell with dividing the sea, but get on
with figuring out a way to multiply the land,"
and how we tried to join him with our shallow
gallows laugh.

Parable

My good neighbor of long standing said to me,
You know, I think that old nursery rhyme,
Row, Row, Row Your Boat, is the golden key
To a successful life. Remember how it goes?

Oh yes, I said, but what about all those folks
Whose boat is leaking, and their oars have
Battered blades and split handles that pinch
Their palms and splinter their fingers at every stroke,
And as far as they can see downstream
There is crashing white water, great boulders
And perhaps a fatal waterfall ahead?

Ah yes, he sighed. I pray for them every day,
I pray earnestly that they can swim—that they
Know how to swim, he said, pouting his lips
Thoughtfully and nodding his white head.
Yes, they must know how to swim.

A Peddler's Prayer

Lord,
It takes a while to find your way
among all the ways of work,
and I suppose a man is never sure.
Take me for example.
I might have taught grammar to freshmen,
history to the cataloging mind,
or journalism to young William Allen Whites.
I considered medicine,
thought of suturing my way across
the ripped and torn pieces of humanity
who bleed out life
in the bucket seats of our auto world.
I even thought of insurance
as a way to save whole families
of widows and orphans.
I could have bought the world with credit cards,
saved the world with green stamps,
given the world away with gift certificates.
I could have sold almost anything.
But,
you called me to be a pastor,
and here I sit among the people—
pushing prayers
swapping jokes
trading self-esteem for longevity
begging for building funds
rustling a Catholic now and then

hawking the urban problem
picking pockets with committee posts
pirating among the open pulpits
auctioning God to the lowest bidder.
Lord,
just exactly what was it you had in mind
when we talked so long ago?
Would you please go over that just one more life,
slowly?
    Amen

Prayer from the Steeple

Lord,
Let's watch things,
you and I
from the grandstand
of this steeple.
We can see it all from here:
the people, houses, traffic
among the cluttered streets
and down the cool boulevards.
Notice how no one looks up?
They surely must know
that we are here, watching,
waiting for them to need us
and return to the altar
that we have kept
polished and dressed
for the season of repentance.
Shall we continue to wait
at this distance?
I could call down to them
and announce a time for prayers.
might even scatter messages
to the street
for them to gather up
like new money
to redeem these sordid days.
I really should go down among them
and bear the cup of cold water
and perhaps the bread.
But the streets are battle lines
and here I am
armed only with the paper word
of the Lord.

Yet, it's marvelous how this tower
gives me a kind of courage.
Thank you, Lord.
Lord?
LORD?
. . . amen.

Pelican

The lone pelican
  fishes just off shore at dawn,
  black wings folding and unfolding
  in slow, low circles,
  eyes out to spot smaller creatures
  surface feeding
  in their calm, glistening sea
  and unaware of hovering wings
  as the pelican folds, pitches forward
  and drops like a rock
  into the bay
  then quickly up again rising dripping
  and gulping breakfast
  of fish also feeding without fear.
Content with his coffee, the old man
  follows nature's random pirating
  and wonders what waits to feed on him
  foraging about in this world's waters
  as he fishes out his life.

Psalm to Warlords Everywhere

Let suns freeze and moons pop
Let tears cut rivers through the ancient soil
Let all springs boil
Let seasons stop
    When I
Let seeds decay and sperm corrupt
Let bombs hatch and praying men spit fire
Let prisoners expire
Let graves erupt
    When I
Let drums sag and gills take air
Let Justice weep and every court be bought
Let love be fought
Let eyes stare
    When I
Let homes be caves and worms be blest
Let peace explode and whispers echo in the world
Let tongues be curled
Let music rest
    When I
Let flags be mops and rain be brine
Let infants enter laughing and honor rot
Let all blood clot
Let yours be mine
    When I

Puzzle Pieces

"We live in two landscapes . . . one that's eternal
and divine, and one that's just the back yard."
—Charles Wright, poet

At eight, I wandered alone in my grandmother's house
while she and my mother were next door having tea.
I pretended I was playing the piano as I fingered the keys.
I searched for my features among photographs
on the mantel, and wondered about lost relatives
saved only in family Bibles.
I found a puzzle box in a glass door bookcase,
and dumped the pieces on the dining room table.

When my mothers returned,
Grandmother stood behind me with her hands
on my shoulders for the longest time before she said,
Son, you can't make that picture because the pieces
are parts of all the puzzles I just couldn't throw away.
And now, eight decades later, I recall only saying, *Oh?*
and memory leaves me today to wonder
if something new, even sublime, might yet be made
with all the leftover pieces of our lives.

The Cow

The cow is now.
Lowing and chewing,
no mewing or bowing to spring
like that upon a rat.
The cow's no cat.
In grass to eat
or stream to drink,
the cow's a statue against the sky.
Her great head still,
her eyes staring at you,
she parks.
A dog remembers you, and barks,
but the vacant-eyed cow is only now.
I mean
she lives right now,
she's in it this minute.
She takes a stand,
and wouldn't give a fig
to do a jig.
The cow's no pig.
Yet, some nights after milking,
soon as the sun sinks and the farm sleeps,
in the lull till dawn
she'll yawn, then take a great run
and sail clear over the moon
like a gull over a dune.
How?
Who knows?
She just says, "NOW!"
and goes.

Requiem

When the rattler bit Tom, our great mule
whinnied in terror and his legs began shaking
into a death dance as he fought going down
and my big brother Ronnie and I slid off his
back, and he killed the snake. We had ridden
Tom down to our back forty to pick a gunny
sack of fresh green corn at our acreage
on the Carolina side of the Savannah River.

Finally, Tom was on the ground and let me
stroke his neck as I waited in a death watch
while Ronnie walked the mile to our house
and Tom was still having spasms when he
returned with our hired man, two shovels
and a small pistol. When he pointed the gun
at Tom's brow, I turned away and jumped
as he fired; then the men began digging
at the near edge of the field.

Back at home, Ronnie nailed the snake through
its battered head to our beech tree in the back
yard, then using a sharp blade, he carefully cut
a red necklace around the snake's neck
and with mouse-nose pliers, peeled off its skin.
After a good scrubbing and a day in the sun
the skin was dry enough for him to begin rubbing
and working it with cotton seed oil until it was
soft and pliable, so he could slide it onto his belt
and wear it off to war in the South Pacific; but I
could never climb that bloodied beech again.

Scaffolding

I read somewhere
That when the George Washington
  monument was under repair,
The metal bar-wrap conjured
  such a vision of pop-art fun
That media reports of protest
  riddled the air
When it came time to remove
  the then useless thing,
For the devoted had fallen in love
  with the scaffolding.

It can also happen otherwise,
  when masks are taken
  for meaning and truth,
Or the poetic original is lost in passion
  for the literal, or deeper
Visions are dismissed if someone chides
  They are only myths.
Yet, for me, my religion is scaffolding
  on which I have grown old
Walking its wobbly boards, building
  a lighthouse for my soul.

Seminary Commencement

O God,
This is a hallelujah night!
We gather to praise learning,
the handling of great problems,
the discovery of ingenious solutions,
the building of word games,
and all the bright distractions
that keep us from wrestling the angel.
We gather to praise the churches,
youth groups and committees,
classes and boards,
who taught us, endured us,
loved and forgave us,
churches of the kingdom
that stand firm despite us.
We gather to praise the people
who pointed the way,
pastors and parents,
teachers in country churches
who study their Bibles with a reading glass,
and begin their giving with a tithe.
O God,
at this new exodus into the world,
we come confessing our accidental discipleship;
our sacrifices have surprised us all,
for we had programmed security.
As we gather to receive the prize,
we know that the diploma and hood
are but paper and cloth,
a far cry from the cross outside.
Nevertheless, we go forth into this world
in which peace has become a mystery to us,
where war is our daily bread
as men grind bone-flour in the military mills.

We go forth into a world in which
brotherhood is a piece of Sunday theatre
when we wear the masks:
white on black,
black on white,
while our hearts are yellowing
with fear of the neighborhood.
Come close now, O Lord,
and do some miracle with us this night,
or tomorrow,
or soon . . .
some miracle, Lord, of peace and love.
In the name of Jesus.
Amen.

Seagull

The seagull
 with a craw for anything
 fishes on acrobatic wings
 closes and dives or rises
 to true cracking heights
dropping shellfish on rocks below
 to feed a ravenous appetite.
He sits for hours
 on his fecal-streaked seawall,
 or stands on a clammy beach
 facing a steady wind of sand
 like a sentinel guarding a lighthouse
 long left on the bank to decay.
But these look-alike, ubiquitous sea birds
 will hear no word of complaint from me,
 even with that squawk
 they do, laughing at me,
 since I also often feel the need
 for their simple, guileless
 anonymity.

Silence

I'll seek out the silence
Of meadows in clover
Of rainbow wet Aprils
With spring running over
    With deer wide awake
    Beneath the tall pine
    As doves nestle down
    Where star-fires shine.

I'll make me a silence
Of language and art
Where poetry and picture
Examine the heart
    As we fashion new gods
    In the image of man
    Makers of mystery
    Now clones of the clan.

I'll find me the silence
Of shrines long in ruin
Where waking the senses
Tops talking and doing
    When listening within
    Brings light for the way
    Where laughter is music
    And passion is play.

I'll turn to that silence
Where love is remembered
Even Golgotha
Cursed and cross-timbered
    Where love all alone
    Told the story of man
    When only God spoke
    And all silence began.

Marriage

Sometimes
  marriage is a great mirage,
  a vision of a Garden of Eden
  where all is hope and promise,
  only to see it turn to sand
  and all the prayers of all the saints
  could not make it the Garden again.
Sometimes
  marriage is a picnic of deli-food and jug wine,
  a leisurely walk beneath the trees, sweet talk
  and long kisses beside the mirror lake,
  with a joy like naked babies in a backyard pool—
  just plain fun.
Sometimes
  marriage is really hard work,
  full of small hurts, sharp words and sudden panic:
  did we choose badly after all?
  has anger ruined a perfect thing?
  did our love wander off and get lost?
  but then we talk, and touch and heal,
  and love again is real,
  and found just sleeping at home all along.
Sometimes
  marriage is a miracle:
  if we get each other loved, everything else
  just seems to fall into place; we talk softer,
  laugh oftener, pray for one another,
  sleep like spoons, say "I'm sorry," forgive quickly,
  keep promises and inquire about each other's soul.

Sometimes
marriage is simply wonderful:
two people who, no matter what comes,
know they want to do life together,
all of it, all the time—the good, bad and ugly—
together, for better or worse,
together . . . forever, in love.
Sometimes
marriage is a legal frame
and the picture is our relationship—
the part that really counts,
because you can have a picture without a frame
but a frame without a picture is empty, useless.
You are love's artists,
and we pray that painting your relationship
will take you a creative lifetime,
and that your picture will be wonderful to behold.

Small Miracle

O God,
My wife
is still the miracle of my life.
She knows how to speak to me
when the world is silent,
and how to remain quiet beside me
when the world is screaming.
She knows my hands and my heart.
She performs magic with my dreams.
Her laughter at my failure is a healing humor
and her tears wash my sin.
She is female joy giving birth to life,
and when all seems success
she reminds me of yesterday's bad judgment
and tomorrow's chance for catastrophe.
She knows that smugness can disarm me
when the work at hand demands
alertness of a mature skepticism.
She is gentle with my fatigue
and honors the strength that survives
the often daunting tasks of manhood.
She prays for me, with me,
but never to me.
I am husband and not God;
and yet she graces this paradise
like a priestess making ritual
of the common life of marriage.
She is love.
She is the mother of our children.
She is home.
Thank you for the miracle of Dian.
Amen.

Speaking of Great Choirs

In Georgia, on a blazing August morning in 1934, I at seven years, was invited to accompany my father in his job traveling from site to site across Bibb County as a Supervisor of Projects for the WPA public works program.

About noon, we arrived at a road construction project, where two long lines of shirtless sweat-slick black men in overalls, with only picks and shovels were carving out a red clay road and singing work-songs broken with *Hunh!* as their picks fell.

When the foreman blew his whistle, they all stopped, walked wearily to a tree shaded hillside, sat in bunches, opened their lard-can tin pails and ate their lunches of fatback and biscuits drizzled with sorghum syrup as water buckets made the rounds.

They motioned me closer while my father took report and gave the foreman envelopes of payday cash. Soon a giant of a man stood and began preaching his shortest sermon, then led this now eager choir of black men in a concert for the trees,

Birds, clouds, surely God and one little white boy, who never heard such singing before or since, and remembers an awakening to the claims of freedom and power in that moment of joy erupting from the hearts of men filled with an ancient jubilation.

Spools

Mother saved her wooden sewing spools,
thread spent patching four sons' trousers, making her
clothes and stitching rag dolls for neighbor girls.
She tossed the spools into a wicker basket
beside her treadle Singer, where they seemed
to take on value for some larger destiny I guessed,
but when I asked, she merely laughed and mentioned
making spool beds—a mystery to me.
Yet, they only collected like the coffee cans, oatmeal boxes
and egg cartons she saved for projects at Sunday School.
Still, I imagined some nobler fate for the spools,
something worthy of their smooth wheeled perfection,
the way I felt the first time I saw a wasting mound
of clam shells, and fretted until I heard they were ground
for calcium—and decided that at least was better than death
as ashtrays I had seen embedded in plaster of Paris alongside
tiny lighthouses in Woolworth's and tourist shops in Atlanta.
Then, during a cold snap one October night
after our father's faithful coal man failed to deliver,
we were down to bedtime huddled in our pajamas
around one of three fireplaces used to heat our home,
And with the last flickering flames only minutes from ashes,
we were suddenly alarmed to see our mother come out
of their bedroom with the full basket of her pristine spools
and with a girlish laugh and a sideways swing, say only
There! and pitch them onto the red-hot bed of coals,
where their quick crackling shattered our silence.

Crocodile

Look closely at the crocodile
  on the bayou or in the Nile
  and you can't miss its Mona Lisa smile
  that's so beguiling,
despite its crusty, scaly skin
  and a whopping tail
  that can do you in.

Now, though it seems absurd
  the crock in some waters
  still has one good friend
  in the tiny, busy plover-bird,
  that pecks vermin from crock's back
  in their codependent life
  like some weird husband and wife
  as strange as any you're apt to see
  of I'll-feed-you-if-you-clean-me.

And while we aren't its natural foes,
  if a sleeping crock looks comatose,
  you'd do well to keep in mind
  this swampy creature
  has one basic feature
  its mammoth mouth can eat'cha
  head to toes.

And come to think of it,
  perhaps that's where the crocodile
  gets its cat-that-ate-the-canary smile.
Oh, and by the way,
  maybe I should also say,
  that you should never try to get away
  with wearing alligator shoes
  on the bayous.

The Big Match

On the fourteenth night in my hospital bed
at the darkest point of my wrestling with COVID,
a rich, deep and comforting voice reminded me
that I still had options, saying matter-of-factly,
"You know, Warren, you don't have to do this—"
not tempting, or suggesting imminent defeat,
but, respecting my autonomy, suggesting to me
that I still had choices, that surrender might even mean
victory. This was the big match and it was half over.
I had only to surrender to my soul's keeper,
the God spirit I knew best, trusted most, loved deepest.
And it was then that I knew for the first time that I
would be going home to finish my journey with
my bride of seventy years just two beds away.

Elephant

The elephant is called a pachyderm
  perhaps because its derm
  is packed solid and firm
  from stem to stern,
  except, of course for those sail-size
  floppy ears and that stringy tail
  for flicking flies giant size.
Land whale among the mammals,
  it rambles and shambles
  though green lush jungles
  stoking its hunk
  with its magical trunk
  that can strip whole trees
  of limbs and leaves;
  or with its prehensile fingerlike
  lips on the tip of its trunk
  feed on tiny berries and seed,
  delicate shoots and roots
  or sniff out fruit
  like the banana
  then shuffles across the savanna
  for an afternoon shower
  under its great trunk tower
  at the favorite watering hole
  preferred by the thundering herd.
And yet,
  we deeply grieve that heartless
  poachers take down this glorious beast
  out of their greedy lust for its ivory tusk,
  and leave it without its family herd
  to die alone.

Mule

In any duel
with a horse
the mule
of course
will lose,
unless you choose
some awful, back-breaking job
like a log-loaded wagon
only a tractor
could pull.
Then the mule
as a rule
will stay the course
to the end
while the horse
will tend
to grouse and pout,
and kick about
and occasionally even pull out
when the going gets tough.
That's when you'll
see the mule
is really a jewel
in the rough
and has the stuff
to stick
and having stuck, ah!
get in the last hee-ha.
The horse adores applause,
while the mule only needs a cause.

USS Thresher

Pod of steel
Resting like a cancer
In the vitals of the earth,
Make peace with us
Who drove you
In our madness there.

Hulk of shame
We take no pride
In your Pyrrhic score
Of depth and speed,
For to go is not enough;
In Holy Week one must return.

Friend of Caesar
You sealed the tomb
In the black week
And Easter barely
Stumbled through the sun
Of our pale hymns.

Man's bleak glory
If you will not come to us
We shall descend to you
And learn the wet truth
Of your retreat
Beyond the clutch of sound.

Missile vault of secrets
We shall diagnose your fault
And create with our hands
Other strong subtombs
Quite large and strong enough
To bury the whole damned world.

Through Galaxies of Love

—poem awaiting its own tune

God's gift of life is in our hands,
Our destiny we form,
The making of tomorrow's dream
Outlives our every storm.
So let us not disown the task,
Nor in our fear decline
The challenge of a global peace
Remains God's grand design.

Our Fatherlands are human pride,
Our quest for power the same.
As children of one God we seek
Love's full-earthly reign,
So let us now all celebrate
The family of Man
And live to help each other live
In every waking land.

The greening of America
Awakes our fantasy,
And dreams of worlds aborning
Challenge old reality.
So let our joy displace all fear,
And raise new symbols high,
A world of candles let us light
To greet the star-flung sky.

To any life alive in space
Inhabiting the spheres
Created by our Father's hand
Beyond the long light years,
We now salute you from our globe
And launch our *Voyager* dove,
As we reach out with prayers for peace
Through galaxies of love.

Toyhood Prayer of a Man

O God,
There is a closet in our bedroom
that leads far back into my toyhood
through pullovers and knickers and broken drums.
It's dark in there.
This stormy night when I am lonely,
when the woman who knows my manhood safe
is away, I close that door carefully, and shut away
the ghosts of prayers drowsily stuck to the dream-end of
sleep. It is not so much that I am afraid to be that boy again.
It's just that things are too common now, too unsingable,
too full of the daily-newspaper stuff of life.
I need the plain joy of make-believe when life was not lived
in tomorrow's planned security, but in the mystery
of today's imagination.
And so, Father, I close the door,
preparing for the day's work ahead,
asking for forgiveness for avoiding mystery and missing a
walk among the fantastic stuffed animals
and bright puzzles
of a world lost in the sullenness of manhood.
Bring the world alive again with fantasy.
Suffer that little child to come unto me.
Amen.

Whatta Ya Say?

If God is that small space
left at the table, then go ahead
and sit there if you like.
Even if you weren't invited,
that doesn't mean you aren't welcome.
Perhaps you were just overlooked,
missed, as in
they would have missed you
and wished you were here
if you hadn't come...
not forgotten
only misplaced when places were set.
Yes, there,
wedge into that spot where John leans away
to rest his head on Jesus . . . right next to Judas,
where you'll have time
to say hello, or even chat a moment,
just small talk you understand
until supper starts.
Whatta ya say?

What Will You Be Doing, God?

What will you be doing, God,
 when I am dying,
 when all sums are tallied,
 when lifetime warranties are running out,
 cherished faces fading,
 dear words sliding into recitation;
 and when I am wanting to rally,
 a last poem is colliding
 with that ancient passion
 for sacred sleep?
What will you be doing, God,
 during the only kiss I ever saved,
 when hands as though my own
 are touching my body's
 prayer places?
What, God, will you be doing
 at journey's end—
 this one that kept folding
 back upon itself in my lostness
 like some newfound, promising route
 this journey
 now running out of road?
God,
 will you be so close
 I cannot see you,
 or so far away that I am left
 with the never-the-less
 of mere surrender, and my own
 bright laughter?

Wintering

It was an overcast late autumn day
With a boisterous wind ripping away last leaves
From already wintering trees to play
A rackety childhood game we called Bank-n-Thieves.

All along our street, the wind was grabbing whole arms full
Of my banked leaves, and sailing away too far to be seen
By these old eyes of one who already feels the awful pull
Of nature that leaves nothing young and green.

Oh yes, the trees will leaf out again, or keep their odds—
Some die—but seasons now revive the ancient myth
Of something clearly awry among the gods
In Paradise, as we must deal with

Out-of-season sub-zero ice and snow
So that instead of sweaters we wear insulated coats;
And if it be my fate that I should go
Where they still separate sheep from goats

I'll hope to be a woolly one who will remain
In a gentle zone of temperate cool
Regardless of the weather, until we perhaps regain
Some hope that seasonal sanity is again the rule.

For now in my own winter, the dark whisper seems
Often at my ear, insisting that I should keep
Preparing for the journey I mostly sense in dreams,
While I remain the weary child fighting sleep.

Woman

—for Mary Dian in celebration of her ninetieth

Woman is mythical as revealed with Eve
and in every culture where honest men
concede to the vast truth of woman's reality.

Woman is mystical with her manifest aura
of the universal, fully present in the moment
while summoning a presence of the eternal.

Woman is magical—menstruating, ovulating
lactating, creating new life as her child is born
more precious to her than herself.

Woman is spiritual, disciple of Psyche, tempted
to be angel; yet, knowing the wisdom of grace,
she creates and nurtures and wisely commands.

And you, my Darling Dian, personify WOMAN
as my intelligent, talented, beautiful, creative,
fun and exciting loving wife and mother Soul Mate,
perfect for me, then, now and always.

I love you so!

Young Theologue

As I stowed my carry-on, I caught the sidelong stare
of a small boy maybe almost four in the window seat
next to mine on the aisle. I gave him a grin as he pumped
up his cheeks until his lips sputtered and squeaked. He
chuckled after the blow, and started another slow pump.

Opening my book, I pretended to ignore him until he asked,
Where you going, Mister? To L.A., I said. We're going to
Los Angeles, he answered, dragging it out. Oh good, I said.
You're on the wrong plane, Mister, and you could get lost.
No, they're the same city, I said.

Just then, a woman across the aisle with twin girls said,
Don't let him bother you; my son's a talker. I can see,
I said, but he's no bother. This is fun. I'm baiting him.
Then eagerly with wide blue eyes, he said, Well . . . if you
do get lost, my mom can find you. She's like God.
She sees everything and finds me all the time, even when
I know where I am. With that, I put down my book
and prepared for dialogue all the way to Los Angeles.

Zebra

Whenever I take the time to read my
horoscope,
and eye the astrological signs,
Libra always reminds me of the Zebra
with its lines,
and of course, it rhymes.
The leopard has spots
and the tiger has stripes
but only the zebra
wears these primordial archetypes
of opposites:
black and white
good and evil
dark and light
day and night
ever moving surreally
through the animal world
in the jungle, on the plain or at the zoo
in a flowing yin-yang harmony,
a visual feast
for both man and beast
as Libra and the zebra
become an equilibrium.

A Living Place

God,
  I'm sure
these sunflower seeds
do not belong in this mayonnaise jar
or even, for that matter,
in the Sears plate-glass bird feeder
on the cedar post above the cats.
They belong in the ground,
in the spring soil
of sun and rain.
Yet, here they are in this dank cellar,
spidered-over, grimy and sooted
from the coal furnace
before its conversion.
I believe that everything wants
a living place,
its home, if you will,
where it becomes what its essence is
at a certain time
and in a certain place.
As, for example, a man
who rests his case for life
upon a sounding place,
a spot on which his life can stand
and from which he can say,
"Here the trembling stops . . . "
Are you, Father,
that living place?
Or is someone screwing the lid down tight,
or, robed and hooded against the winter world,
taking us to the feeder?
Amen.

If God Is this Battered Basin

If God is this battered basin
    carried down the aisle
    in my grandmother's hands,
    towel over her arm,
    walking with the singing,
  "Shall we gather at the river?"
    a capella in this Freewill Baptist Church
    near Macon in 1934;

If God is this tin pan
    she fills from a white pitcher
    while kneeling at the front pew
    weeping and washing her neighbor's
    calloused, hard-nail feet:
    my Grandma,
    with her waterfall tears tumbling
    into Sister Ella's hands, cupped,
    cradled to catch the Spirit;

Then
    wash me now also, God,
    in this memory pan,
    Grandson recalling Grandma
    brought to footwashing
    for who-knows-what small sins
    of gossip or forgetfulness
    and her persistent need
    to get right with God;
    wash me, who walked on without her
    but always with this vision of her
    doing what her Lord did,

because she hurt so
and because she and Sister Ella
needed to cry together
and embrace each other
and give each other a holy kiss
as now when Ella stands, then kneels
to wash my grandmother's feet
in their shared water,
in that battered basin
of God's love.

Signs of Spring

The ubiquitous trifling crows come tripping
  in and out over two wooing doves
  fluttering about,
  but still under the over-flight
  of a young peregrine falcon
  itching to test his talons.
Jays arrive at the feeder pestering the sparrows
  and occasionally,
  even the jumping, snapping dog next door.
I dust off a snow-strewn iron chair
  and drop a warmer cushion there,
  to sit sipping coffee before a hot oatmeal
  and blueberry breakfast, but nearly spoil it
  imagining some waking still-sleepy snake
  uncoiling from his hole to snatch up
  and swallow a careless rodent creeping
  around scratching for acorns and roots
  under our deck.
The dirty lingering snow melts
  in scattered patches over the lawn.
Tulips top the ugly matted winter grass,
  and the faithful golden daffodils arrive
  nodding and waving in the breeze
  to old Bill Wordsworth trudging along
  our path on his staff,
  while one glorious cardinal sits
  for the longest time
  in our Globe Locust lusting for a mate
  and singing spring in.

Slingshot

Few green growing things were less loved
  in the South of my childhood
  than the chinaberry tree with its eager-to-grow
  pithy cane-wood that was good for not
  much more than giving shade
  in a henpecked sandy yard
  where little thrived except kudzu
  that could devour my tree house
  fast as the rattler a careless mouse.
Yet, each spring, when I hacked a fork
  from the chinaberry's tender limbs,
  sliced strips of skin from an old inner tube
  and ripped the tongue out of a wasted shoe
  to make my summer slingshot
  I always felt a tinge of guilt.
Not a lot, you understand, but
  with broken rules
  and a few simple sins, just enough
  to keep me submissively in Sunday School,
  or startling myself awake if I forgot
  my prayers before sleep.
Then,
  one night, feeling yet again I had broken
  whichever commandment not to kill,
  I recalled David, the shepherd boy,
  slaying Goliath, then later happily singing
  his psalm about how
  the Lord was his Shepherd,
  knowing full-well this thing
  that he had done
  and where he had cut the hide
  for his deadly sling.
  And I cried.

If God Is Eternal Thou

If God is Eternal Thou,
not you nor I nor we
but utterly Other
wholly beyond knowing
except
as God allows
along all the paths out and away
from Thou to me for me to see
taste touch smell
all that smarts, soothes, quickens,
awakens—
God up close
seeing me touching ecstasy
tasting at the elemental core
smelling my way like a cat
to the fecund delicious fruit
of earth sea and sky,
chewing leafy life
loving this rising ache of longing,
arriving prepared to leave
dreaming against nightmares that haunt
this weak heartbeat of hope,
dreaming, always dreaming toward life
toward you
God,
Thou outloud!
Listen to that sound
out of the slumbering skull
just before first dawn.

Thou!
    How art Thou now,
    now that I know your name?
You are known.
I am mystery.
We are one.

A Friend's Dream on Good Friday

You shared a dream that constellated your fear
of knives, since that childhood switchblade
thing—dreaming of a drawer of kitchen knives,
that somehow felt right to you on the day of spikes,
thorns and spears, and you knew what it meant.

One knife offered nothing to you, with its simple
stock handle, its nice little heft and the sharp edge
of a tidy well-honed carving knife to be holstered
in its block.

But the next was double-edged, cutting both ways
and flashing as though bent on persuading you—
we decided—to shed your dithering with those
precious doubts of yours longtime withering.

A third was a battered, crescent-worn oyster knife,
offering to pry open your steely resolve never
to risk your life with a daunting new deed or devotion
beyond changing doctors or cities or wives.

The last at first seemed to be just a dull butcher blade
until you whet-stoned it to a keen point and with
the insouciant trust of a sous chef's art, you thrust it
home, so that your water-logged, and barnacled
limping-along heart left you believing that one day
you would have what you've never known—
awaking to a resurrection morning all your own.

Loves

I have loved many women, young and old,
a number of interesting men, lots of children,
one sweet shepherd dog when I was a boy,
scores of poems, books and Schubert's music.

I have loved a few special paintings, sculptures,
the dark heart of a pine forest, my birthday beech,
a rich Cabernet in a swirly-blue hand-blown glass
the day I resigned from a mulish faculty.

I have loved our children dancing around the tree
on a long-ago Christmas night, one well-earned
knee scar from sliding into second, a backyard tree
of ripe, waspy figs, and our clock striking right now.

I have loved snagging a water moccasin swimming
upstream and scaring the fish into hiding in a black
swamp Georgia stream, then hanging him headless
on a limb to dry when I was ten and lord of the flies.

I have loved again and again the day I came home to you
from Korea and found our love still alive and daring us
to live at the heart of our great passion, even with both
of us scared yet ready to embrace our shining new world.

I have loved you and your blue eyes over these many years
with the deepest love I know—my best heart, mind
and my poor soul and even with
the worst of me.

Shine

In Charleston on a Sunday,
I took a rare step for me
and climbed into an old, gray Shoeshine's chair,
pulled my trousers up to my sock tops
and said, "These are old and cheap, but see
if you can put a shine on a J.C. Penny original
after a little gloss from me over the years."
With a grin and a Gulla-Geechee low-country patois,
he said, "Shoes is shoes, but these doan look like
trav'lin shoes to me. How long yo say?"
"Ten maybe fifteen years."
"Shux, that ain't old from here. You wanna see old?"
and he lifted his foot like a horse for shoeing,
so I could see it smudge-black, battered
with a hole to the skin.
"And you a Shoeshine," I teased.
"Yessiree," he bragged, "But I bet my shoes
been happier places than yo's."
"Probablee," I said going along and wondering
but not asking and neither of us offering more.
He started humming to himself just when
it could have gotten good, and after all the
rubbing, shining and popping his rag,
he tapped my sole and said, "Thas the bess I can do
fo' fi-dollar," and smiled big as life.
I paid him well and stepped down:
"Thank you for the tip," I said,
and he winked with a grin.

Poem for You

My poem is a kiss
  searching for direction,
  going as far as it dreams
  towards something or someone
that's always waiting . . .

  my fingertips kissed
  and tossed upon the air
  for your lips only—
someone's always waiting . . .

Kiss for a poem arriving late,
  wineglass with your lipstick print,
  chalice at our own altar—
someone always waiting . . .

Orange slices, bare legs, an ear
  that rings when kissed, eyelids,
  your dangling earrings removed—
someone's always waiting . . .

Ripe figs, a fine Bordeaux
  saved for this feast day,
  your breast, nest and all the rest—
something's always waiting . . .

Then some things leave and go away,
  even love poems like this one I'm sure
  I'm losing now with all my baiting
before I saw that your are waiting.

My Father Dying

In his stories and the scriptures he quotes
fall gods and lucifers,
lie trolls and tramps,
burn saints and witches
a royalty and rabble of archetypes.
He mimics their death rattle in coliseum.
He sings to his nurses above the hiss
of the first singeing tongues leaping
at the throat of Great John Huss, his kind of man.
He walks with Dylan's father going gentle,
arguing with rage,
whispering, "Kiss the scythe."
He sanctifies the bed sheets with his blood.
He sleeps in the garden with Peter.
He is my father dreaming of dying on his pilgrim feet,
in that shining line
above the mob,
embracing death like a brother,
knowing there is a marker
in place beside my mother,
without tribute or inscription,
bearing only his name and birth,
the last date in ancient numerals yet to be carved
into his headless stone.

Morning

Morning always seems to arrive full of itself,
dragging dream's delights and disasters
like a child her battered and beloved
ragdoll by its one reliable arm
to breakfast.
Morning tilts toward waking
like her old, slow-rising grandpa
making his way on his cane
down the hall toward breaking news,
then turning away
out to the patio instead
with its table waiting, baiting him
with a sparkling white bowl
of ripe, red plums
and signs of the sun.
And there they will find each other,
the wrinkled leftovers of night past
and the expectant bright face
of a new day, still believing
each will be there waiting,
knowing they must meet
for their very own silly daydream
of something simply wonderful.

Smithy

James Alfred Lane was a big man,
with coal-black curly hair, fair complexion and blue eyes
and the only blacksmith in Griffin, Georgia, in 1931
when I was four. He was my grandpa, and I loved
him. On the way to board our train, my older brother
Ronnie and I stopped by his shop to say goodbye.

Across the broad clinker floor, we saw him
nailing shoes on a great brown stallion, and when
the horse tried to jerk his leg away, Grandpa just
yanked back and kept nailing until he was done,
then looked up and smiled. Oh yes, he said, going
home day isn't it? Well, we really enjoyed you boys
this summer and we'll miss you for sure. In his
leather apron, and still holding his hammer, he said,
Well, bye now, and turned away rubbing a fist across,
his eyes, and when he called out Love you,
we echoed back to him, Love you too,
as we closed the giant rolling door behind us.

He would never have said it, but he was an artist,
Making fancy wrought iron ornamental yard pieces, and
selling them all the way to Charleston. Once when my
mother complimented him on a new creation,
he looked down and said, It's my soul work you know,
the Lord's in it . . . at least for me he is.

Paper Bells

O God,
How does a man repair a tattered joy,
a shrill peep deep in the throat
at the squeak of the first snow
a banter with a loose bird
escaped in the living room of canary cages
set open to Christmas
a laughter lost in a cigar box of bright tree lights?
Where is the whistling?
Where is the tinseled, holly throat
of a boy singing his way up the azalea aisle
to the dark kings kneeling before the creche-child
Jenny's plastic doll under a blue spot?
I volunteered to play shepherd.
I bought a new flannel robe
and crooked a sapling from the vacant lot next door.
I even bound my thinning hair in a woman's scarf
and practiced kneeling for the first time
since the eve of my wedding day.
I laughed aloud at rehearsal,
suggesting that a small boy
could better guide the deacons through the dark
to find the star hanging among the organ pipes.
Then
a carol began from the throat of a cherub-child,
my son, my own surprise son
a stand-in angel called from the wings of boyhood
to sing down the silent night,
calling his father to bright tears.
Thank you for the joy that rang the paper bells!
Amen.

Missouri and Kaw

The rivers float the fables
of twin towns buried
upon the banks
of a brown-mud time
when alleys puddled pigs,
and cattle thundered yards
into a storm of wealth,
while cowboys wet down
dust with whiskey.
The rivers dredge in decay,
and wedge through glass and steel
with a pitiful sucking for life,
slipping through the sewers
of our wasted dreams
piled one upon another
in growing decades
of urban pillage
and Christian enterprise.

Who Called?

Dear God,
When the long search for the right time
had crossed from sky to earth
and the boy was lost in his bright climb
to noon
with sun flashing
on all the golden leaves of youth,
who called him
from this first, brief spell of glory
before the sherry-scented mothers
and tobacco-tweed fathers
grinning beyond the footlights?
Who called him
to the stale view of childhood
tortured by our broken promises
still blocked and brown
upon the rooftops of our aimless parenthood
like fading papers that missed the porches?
Who called him for one moment to all of this,
and why did he forget his lines so perfectly?
Amen.

Love Feast

Then there are all our foods of love: fruits, nuts,
Herbs, peppers, sea salt, beans, greens and grains,
Wines, liquors, creams, vinegars and virgin olive oil,
Milk and cheeses, magic potions, philters and powders
With harder delectables needing pestle and mortar
Among a stash of mixers, measures and keeping-jars,
An assortment of cup, bowl, glass and plate
Even coin silver hand-to-mouth utensils along with
A gathering store of old menus and recipes begged,
Borrowed and pilfered here and there for special
Gourmet feasts of love in sweet variety, such as:

Scuppernongs plucked sunny warm from the vine,
Peking liquor, nut and pomegranate gold, hot
Buttered oysters, painted cups of coddled eggs,
Duck with chocolate sauce, bananas flambé,
Our own crisp sugar cookies for nibbling,
A Casanova snack of prosciutto between two
Slices of Roquefort bedded in thin broad cuts
Of multi-grain German brown bread, best melted,
Ginseng soup with chrysanthemums, peaches
In red wine, Belle Helene pears with vanilla ice,
Prawns in ginger sauce, Greek yogurt with figs
And honey, fish with bamboo shoots, she-crab soup,
Fresh clams and eels with cockle bread, best eaten
Near or in rich recall of the smell and sound of the sea.

Yet, my dear, to what end is all our feasting
Unless I taste you and you taste me?

If God Is a Diviner

If God is a diviner
  teasing like a water witch
  dowsing the inner dark
  with his witch hazel switch
  to find water beneath dry ground,
  perhaps she can divine
  my wellspring with her wand,
  find the vein
  that coils and creeps
  in the eternal deep
  where only nature can find nature
  and only the holy meets soul,
  and I can again be certain of her
  as an old rock knows its underwetness,
  an empty womb believes in sudden fruit,
  and the dark moon expects light
  each night . . .
  and a fountain will begin in me
  as sweat,
  and I shall begin to dig.

Life Signs

—in memory of my mother on Mother's Day, 2010

My mother saved everything:
a pin she wore on her wedding day
with three of its cluster of rhinestones
missing,
too precious to repair and wear;

her father's pocket knife, one bone-side
missing
and its best blade tip snapped;

a ribbon she wore at eight the day
her mother went to see Jesus,
too sick to say goodbye;

her Bible with its pressed and faded red rose
from the casket spray, the day she could not
cry, but wept dry tears the rest of her life;

an inch-long thin white scar
on her left thumb she sliced with a hatchet
as a girl splitting kindling wood for the stove,
that her gentle blacksmith father sewed up
with a silk thread while she sat on the stump
like a good girl and watched without a peep;

a penny I swallowed when I was three,
my first baby tooth
and the first poem she taught me
from the Macon *Telegraph* that I have
saved for her all these years
to recite to you in case you ask.

You

I do wish I could find a way
to fit you into my schedule.
There just never seems to be
enough of anything—
faith, hope or love,
but surely most of all,
time.
It takes time, I find,
to acquire the others,
so finding time for you
who bring none of these
with you
when we do lunch
just might explain
why, when you complain,
my book is full
of those who bring
the next best thing
to the table: gossip.
So, there you have it.
It's really not about time,
is it?
It's finally still about you,
after all.

If God Is Tree Roots in Our Garden

If God is the great tree roots
  of oak, elm, ash and sweet gum
  burrowing deep in our garden,
  which like their branches above
  reach to seek the sun
  and slowly root upward,
  shouldering loose the stepstones
  across the lawn
  laid long ago and meant to stay,
  now making my way impossible;
Then
  I accept the message
  and leave them raised
  like unsettled tombstones
  to remind me that God
  may move slowly to undo
  all familiar paths
  with nothing more to mark the way
  than the trail I leave
  with my own faint dewprints
  on the grass.

If God Is this Last Snowman

If God is this last snowman
    before spring,
    rolled and raised in the image of man
    standing now in my dead garden
    like frozen Adam looking lost
    trying to recall the names
    of plants withered under snow,
    animals burrowed in,
    birds flown;
Then
    I will wait
    for the sun to come
    and melt us both,
    him down to bulbs and roots,
    me out of doors
    into the waking garden
    where I will watch
    for signs of those
    returning to this place
    as though called
    even though not one of them
    knows its name.

Eulogy for John Keats

Thirty has always been my most daunting birthday.
It crept toward me like an enemy one fears,
For though I had poems published here and there,
At my age, Keats was already dead five years.

Keats and his three siblings were orphaned young
With John in the role of older devoted brother
To George, Tom and Fanny with meager financial aid
And the prospect of tubercular deaths like their mother.

As a school boy, Keats was a fearsome scrapper
Although or because he never grew above five feet;
Yet, he was well built, handsome and a fine scholar
Steeped in Shakespeare, Milton, Latin and Greek.

At about nineteen he pledged himself *to do the work*
His soul decreed. His juvenilia, like most, were derived,
But soon his own distinctive patterns, images and idioms
Appeared in letter-poems and gifts to friends, until arrived.

His sonnet, "On First Looking into Chapman's Homer,"
With its marked economy and brilliant imagery, a signet test
For any poet, that sustained its magic through fourteen lines
Which set him apart as one contending with England's best,

As are his amazing letters full of profound ideas and charm,
Where, leading like a pole star, is his belief that in this life
We are here to grow a Soul. He fell in love with Fanny Brawn,
But his failing health prevented her from becoming his wife.

He published books of poems and endured hateful reviews,
But kept writing with the conviction that poetry was his destiny.
Ill and drifting toward death, his amazing poems continued down
To his last great odes composed like symphonies toward eternity.

Yet, success came too late for him to know he had entered
Our Pantheon of Poets, and his humility of the first order
Led him to insist that the inscription on his tombstone read,
"Here Lies One Whose Name Was Writ in Water."

Moon Prints

The racing river holds in place
  the moon coin fumbling on its face,
  bubbling in glints,
  bouncing on chattering rivulets
  in the stream and shattering
  the distant image into bits,
  yet holding its phantom light
  arriving here off lunar scar-fields
  sending, if we could only see,
  water pixels of tiny distant footprints
  like dancing angels
  etched on the head of a pin.

Going

Don't know where I'm going
don't know how I'll get there
not sure where I'll be when I arrive,
but I'm still going
still moving on
living like a king while I'm alive.

Don't know when I'm leaving
whether night or day
not sure I'll be ready when it's time,
but I'm still going
still moving on
living like a king to my last dime.

Don't know how I'll leave here
sick or in my prime
not sure what I'll be wearing when I depart,
but I'm still going
still moving on
living like a king with my sweetheart.

Don't know if I'll go alone
or if some other soul
will be ready and willing to go along,
but I'm still going
still moving on
perhaps I'll sing to the King my last song.

About the Author

95 at 95 is Dr. Warren Lane Molton's fourth volume of poetry: *Bruised Reeds* was published in 1970, *If God Is* in 2002, and *New Poems, 2002–2012* in 2012. He is also the author of two books on couple relationships: *Friends, Partners and Lovers* and *Spheres of Intimacy*. Dr. Molton was in private practice for more than forty-five years as a pastoral counselor specializing in individual, couple, group, and family therapy. He was the director and co-founder of the Counseling Center for Human Development in Kansas City, Missouri, until his retirement in 2020.

Dr. Molton holds graduate degrees from Yale Divinity School and Chicago Theological Seminary. He pastored churches, served as a military chaplain in Korea, and was a campus minister at the University of Connecticut and a professor of pastoral theology at Central Baptist Theological Seminary. He is past poetry editor of *Pilgrimage, The Journal of Existential Psychology*, and has lectured and led workshops on adult relational life and the use of poetry for spiritual growth and healing. He has been married for seventy-three years to Mary Dian Molton, a retired Jungian therapist and author of *Four Eternal Women: Tony Wolff Revisited—A Study in Opposites* and *About Franz*, which recounts her friendship with Carl Jung's eldest son.

www.ingramcontent.com/pod-product-compliance
Lightning Source LLC
LaVergne TN
LVHW051006080826
845145LV00009B/2493

* 9 7 8 1 9 5 6 0 5 6 9 7 6 *